Best Known Latin Songs

Piano • Vocal • Guitar

S0-AKD-372

Contents

ISBN 0-7935-1942-X

This publication is not for sale in the EC and/or Australia or New Zealand.

HAL•LEONARD CORPORATION

7777 W. BLUEMOUND RD. P.O. BOX 13819 MILWAUKEE, WI 53213

AMOR EM PAZ
(Once I Loved) (Love In Peace)

Words and Music by ANTONIO CARLOS JOBIM
and VINICIUS DE MORAES

3

ARRIVEDERCI ROMA
(From The Motion Picture "SEVEN HILLS OF ROME")

Words by CARL SIGMAN
Music by R. RASCEL

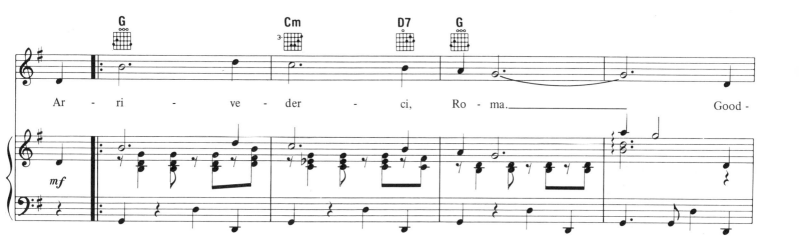

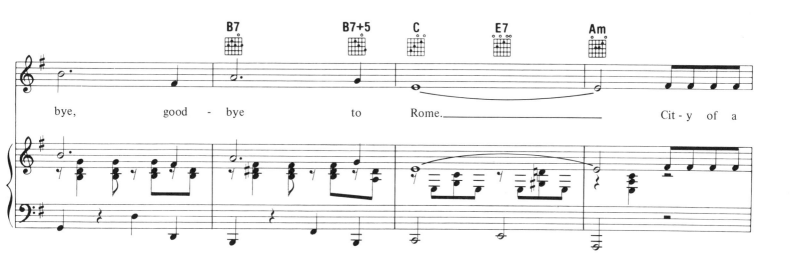

ANEMA E CORE
(With All My Heart)

English Lyric by CURTIS MANN
and HARRY AKST
Italian Lyric by TITO MANLIO
Music by SALVE D'ESPOSITO

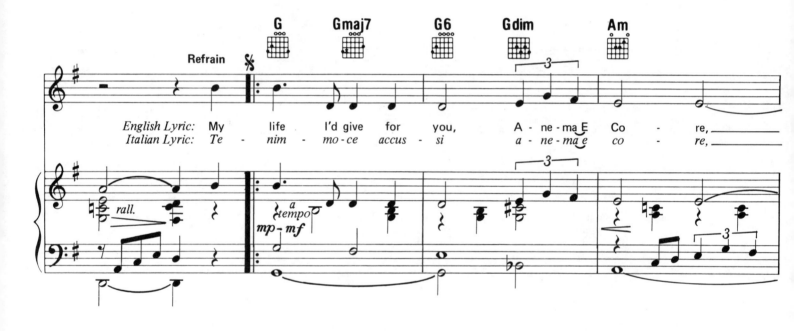

English Lyric: My life I'd give for you, A - ne-ma E Co - re,_____
Italian Lyric: Te nim - mo-ce accus - si a - ne-ma e co - re,_____

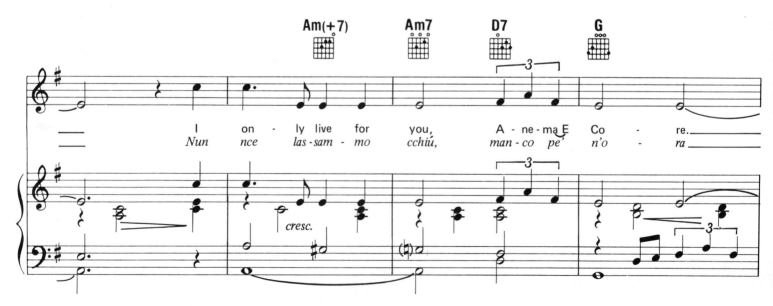

I on - ly live for you, A - ne-ma E Co - re._____
Nun nce las-sam - mo cchiú, man - co pe' n'o - ra_____

MCA music publishing

ANNA
(EL NEGRO ZUMBON)
From the film "ANNA"

English lyric by WILLIAM ENGVICK
Original Text by F. GIORDANO;
Music by R. VATRO

Original Lyric by F. Giordano

Ya viene el negro zumbón bailando alegre el baión,
repica la zambumba y llama la mujer. *(repeat)*

Tengo gana de bailar el nuevo compas.
Dicen todos cuando me veen pasar:
Chica, donde vas? Me voy pa' bailá el baión.
Tengo gana de bailar el nuevo compas.
Dicen todos cuando me veen pasar:
Chica, donde vas? Me voy pa' bailá el baión.

APPLES AND BANANAS

By FRANK SCOTT

Moderately

CHERRY PINK AND
APPLE BLOSSOM WHITE

French Words by JACQUES LARUE
English Words by MACK DAVID
Music by LOUIGUY

It's cher-ry pink and ap-ple blos-som white,__ When your true lov-er comes your way.
cher-ry tree.__ Be-side an ap-ple tree did grow.

It's cher-ry pink and ap-ple blos-som white,__ The po-ets
And there a boy once met his bride to be__ long long a-

say. The sto-ry goes that once a go
The boy looked

A DAY IN THE LIFE OF A FOOL
(Manhá De Carnaval)

Words by CARL SIGMAN
Music by LUIZ BONFA

Slow Bossa Nova

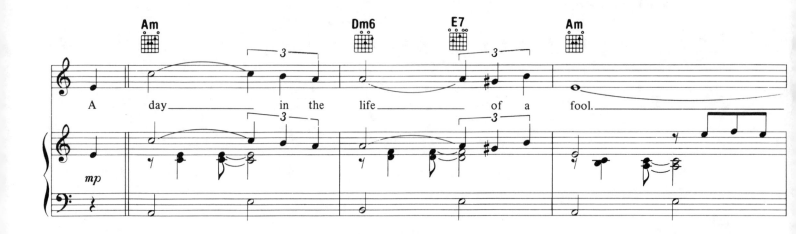

A day _____ in the life _____ of a fool. _____

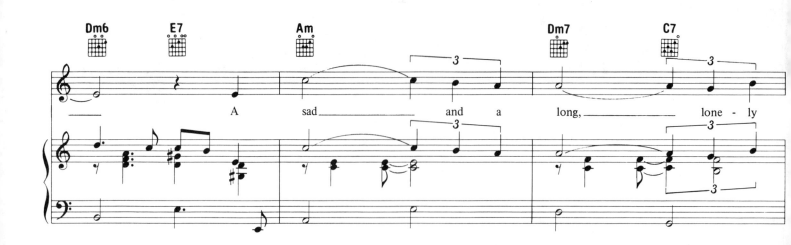

_____ A sad _____ and a long, _____ lone-ly

THE END OF A LOVE AFFAIR

Words and Music by
EDWARD C. REDDING

24

FLY ME TO THE MOON
(In Other Words)

Words and Music by
BART HOWARD

I GET IDEAS

Words by DORCAS COCHRAN
Music by JULIO C. SANDERS

When we are danc- ing and you're dan- ger- ous- ly near me, I get i-

deas, ___ I get i- deas. ___ I wan- na hold you so much clos- er than I

dare to, I wan- na scold you 'cause I care more than I care to. And when you

THE GIRL FROM IPANEMA
(Garôta De Ipanema)

Original Words by VINICIUS DE MORAES
English Words by NORMAN GIMBEL
Music by ANTONIO CARLOS JOBIM

MCA music publishing

I TALK TO THE TREES
(From "PAINT YOUR WAGON")

Words by ALAN JAY LERNER
Music by FREDERICK LOEWE

IN THE STILL OF THE NIGHT

Words and Music by
COLE PORTER

IT'S IMPOSSIBLE
(SOMOS NOVIOS)

English Lyric by SID WAYNE
Spanish Words and Music by A. MANZANERO

It's im-pos-si-ble, tell the
So-mos no-vios pues los

sun to leave the sky, it's just im-pos-si-ble.
dos sen-ti-mos mu tuo_a-mor pro-fun-do

It's im-pos-si-ble, ask a
Y con e-so ya ga-

52

JALOUSIE
(JEALOUSY)

Music by JACOB GADE
Words by VERA BLOOM

LA PALOMA

English Lyrics by MARJORIE HARPER
Music by D. DE YRADIER
Arranged by R. ROSAMOND JOHNSON

60

2.

I'll give you my hand, with all of the love I own;

I'll live all my life for you and you alone;

We'll go to church for blessings that wait in store,

And so - there'll be one where two had been before.

3.

The day we are married, we'll tell the world "Goodbye,"

Away we will go together, you and I.

But when time has passed us by with each coming year,

'Tis then, many little Gauchos will appear.

2.
El dia que nos casemos
Valgamé Dios!
En la semana que hay ir
Me hace reir
Desde la Yglesia juntitos
Que si senor
Nos hiremos a dormir
Alla voy yó
Si a tu ventana llega etc.

3.
Cuando el curita nos seche
La bendicion
En la Yglesia Catrédal
Alla voy yó
Yo te daré la manita
Con mucho amor
Y el cura dos hisopazos
Que si senor
Si a tu ventana llega etc.

LITTLE BOAT
(O BARQUINHO)

Original Words by RONALDO BOSCOLI
English Words by BUDDY KAYE
Music by ROBERTO MENESCAL

Moderately

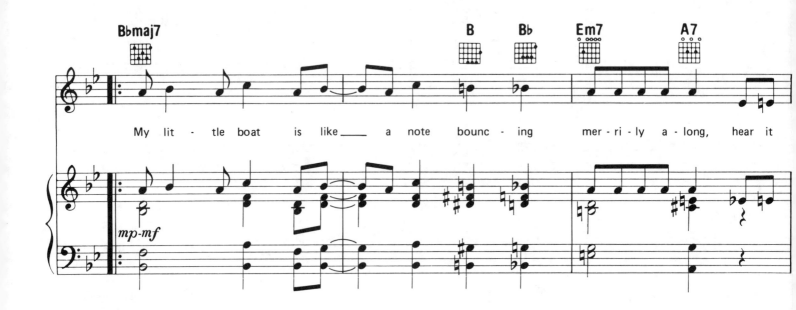

My lit-tle boat is like___ a note bounc-ing mer-ri-ly a-long, hear it

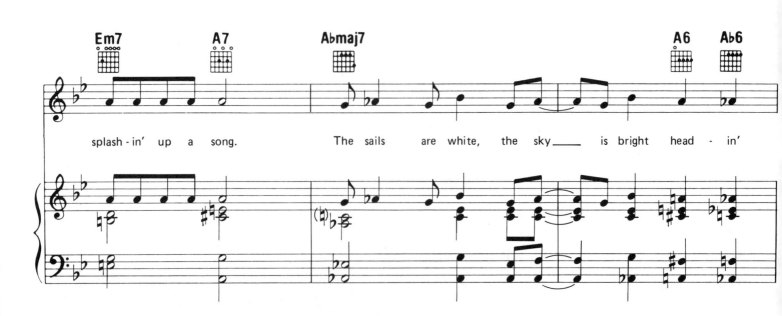

splash-in' up a song. The sails are white, the sky___ is bright head-in'

MCA music publishing

64

A MAN AND A WOMAN
(Un Homme Et Une Femme)

Original Words by PIERRE BAROUH
English Words by JERRY KELLER
Music by FRANCIS LAI

67

MEDITATION
(Meditacáo)

English Words by NORMAN GIMBEL
Original Words by NEWTON MENDONCA
Music by ANTONIO CARLOS JOBIM

MCA music publishing

70

MIAMI BEACH RUMBA

Words by ALBERT GAMSE
Music by IRVING FIELDS

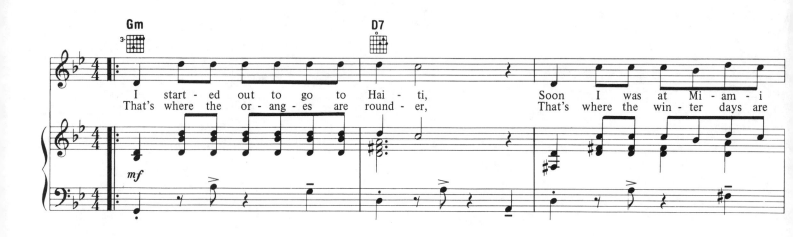

I start - ed out to go to Hai - ti,
That's where the or - ang - es are round - er,
Soon I was at Mi - am - i
That's where the win - ter days are

Beach.
warm.
There, not so ver - y far from Hai - ti,
That's where I caught a hun - dred pound - er,

MORE
(Theme From "MONDO CANE")

English Words by NORMAN NEWELL
Music by RIZ ORTOLANI
and NINO OLIVIERO

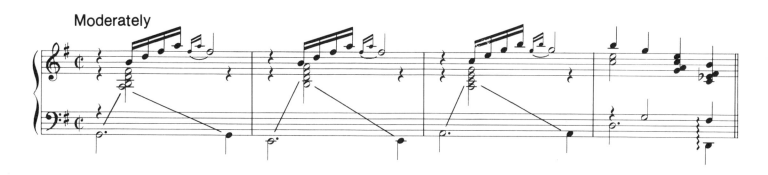

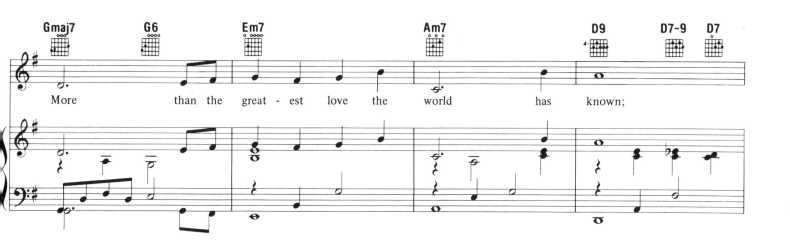

More than the great-est love the world has known;

This is the love I'll give to you a - lone.

NEVER ON SUNDAY

(From Jules Dassin's Motion Picture "NEVER ON SUNDAY")

Words by BILLY TOWNE
Music by MANOS HADJIDAKIS

ONE NOTE SAMBA
(Samba De Uma Nota So)

Original Lyrics by NEWTON MENDONCA
English Lyrics by ANTONIO CARLOS JOBIM
Music by ANTONIO CARLOS JOBIM

Lightly, with movement

This is just a lit-tle sam-ba built up-on a sin-gle note.

O-ther notes are bound to fol-low but the root is still that note.

Now the new one is the con-se-quence of the one we've just been throug

QUIET VILLAGE

Lyric by MEL LEVEN
Music by LESLIE BAXTER

ORCHIDS IN THE MOONLIGHT

Words by GUS KAHN
and EDWARD ELISCU
Music by VINCENT YOUMANS

Lyrics:

When or-chids bloom in the moon - light ___ and lov-ers vow to be true, ___ I still can dream in the moon - light

Of one dear night that we knew. ___ When or-chids fade in the dawn - ing, ___

___ They speak of tears and "Good - bye!" ___ Tho' my dreams are shat-tered Like the pet - als scat-tered,

OUR DAY WILL COME

Words by BOB HILLIARD
Music by MORT GARSON

Slowly, with expression

MCA music publishing

OUR LANGUAGE OF LOVE

Music by MARGUERITE MONNOT
Original French words by
ALEXANDRE BREFFORT
English words by JULIAN MORE,
DAVID HENEKER and MONTY NORMAN

POINCIANA
(Song Of The Tree)

Words by BUDDY BERNIER
Music by NAT SIMON

QUANDO, QUANDO, QUANDO
(TELL ME WHEN)

Italian Words by A. TESTA
English Words by PAT BOONE
Music by TONY RENIS

QUIET NIGHTS OF QUIET STARS
(CORCOVADO)

English Words by GENE LEES
Original Words and Music by ANTONIO CARLOS JOBIM

Qui - et nights of qui - et stars,

MCA music publishing

SAMBA DE ORFEU

Words by ANTONIO MARIA
Music by LUIZ BONFA

SOMEONE TO LIGHT UP MY LIFE

(Se Todos Fossem Iguais A Voce)

English Lyric by GENE LEES
Original text by VINICIUS de MORAES
Music by ANTONIO CARLOS JOBIM

Moderate Bossa Nova

Go on your way _____ with a cloud-less blue sky a-bove, _____
Vae tua vi-da _____ Teu ca-mi-nho é de paz e a-mor. _____

_____ may all your days _____ be a won-der-ful
_____ A tua vi-da _____ Eu u-ma lin-da can-

song of love. _____ O-pen your arms and
cão de a-mor; _____ A-bre teus bra-ços e

SOUTH OF THE BORDER
(Down Mexico Way)

By JIMMY KENNEDY
and MICHAEL CARR

114

SPEAK LOW
(From "ONE TOUCH OF VENUS")

Words by OGDEN NASH
Music by KURT WEILL

116

SPANISH EYES

Words by CHARLES SINGLETON
and EDDIE SNYDER
Music by BERT KAEMPFERT

SUMMER SAMBA
(So Nice)

Original Words and Music by MARCOS VALLE
and PAULO SERGIO VALLE
English Words by NORMAN GIMBEL

122

SUMMERTIME IN VENICE

English Words by
CARL SIGMAN
Music by ICINI

MCA music publishing

TRISTE

By ANTONIO CARLOS JOBIM

Sad_ is to live in sol - i - tude _____

far_ from your tran - quil al - ti - tude. _____

Portuguese Lyrics:

Triste é viver a na solidão
Na dor cruel de uma paixão
Triste é saber que ninguem pade viver de ilusão
Que nunca vai ser, nunca dar
O sonhador tem que acordar.

Tua beleza é um auião
Demals pra um pobre coracao
Que para pra te ver passar
So pra se maltratar
Triste é viver na solidãd.

WATCH WHAT HAPPENS

English Words by NORMAN GIMBEL
Music by MICHEL LEGRAND

WAVE
(VOU TE CONTAR)

Words and Music by
ANTONIO CARLOS JOBIM

two can dream a   dream to - geth - er. _____

WHAT A DIFF'RENCE A DAY MADE

Lyric by STANLEY ADAMS
Music by MARIA GREVER

YELLOW DAYS
LA MENTIRA (SE TE OLVIDA)

English lyric by ALAN BERNSTEIN
Music and Spanish lyric by ALVARO CARRILLO

With an easy flow

(English) I re-
(Spanish) Se te ol-

mem - ber when the sun - light had a spe - cial kind of
vi - da que me quie - res a pe - sar de lo que

bright - ness, and the laugh - ter held a lov - er's kind of
di - ces, pues lle - va - mos en el al - ma ci - ca-

142

Life is emp - ty ___ and the
De me par - te ___ te de -

sun - light seems so harsh in - stead of ten - der, ___ and the
vuel - vo tu pro - me - sa de a - do - rar - me ___ ni si -

laugh - ter's just an ech - o I re - mem - ber (from) yel - low days, ___ yel - low
quie - ra sien - tas pe - na por de - jar - me que e - se pac - to no es con

days.
dios.

I re - days. _____
Se te ol dios. _____

8va bassa

THE DEFINITIVE COLLECTIONS...

The Definitive Broadway Collection

This is simply the best and most comprehensive collection of Broadway music ever arranged in a piano/vocal format! 142 of the greatest show tunes ever compiled into one volume. This is one book that every Broadway lover must have! Songs include: Don't Cry For Me Argentina • Hello, Dolly! • I Dreamed A Dream • Lullaby Of Broadway • Mack The Knife • Memory • Send In The Clowns • Somewhere • The Sound Of Music • Strike Up The Band • Summertime • Sunrise, Sunset • Tea For Two • Tomorrow • What I Did For Love • more.

00359570 ....$27.95

The Definitive Country Collection

A must-own collection of over 90 country classics, including: Coward Of The County • Crazy • Daddy Sang Bass • Forever And Ever, Amen • Friends In Low Places • God Bless The U.S.A. • Grandpa (Tell Me About the Good Old Days) • Help Me Make It Through The Night • I Was Country When Country Wasn't Cool • I'm Not Lisa • I've Come To Expect It From You • I've Cried My Last Tear For You • Luckenbach, Texas • Make The World Go Away • Mammas Don't Let Your Babies Grow Up To Be Cowboys • Okie From Muskogee • Tennessee Flat Top Box • Through The Years • Where've You Been • and many more

00490195 ....$24.95

The Definitive Jazz Collection

A once-in-a-lifetime collection of 90 of the greatest jazz songs ever compiled into one volume. Includes: Ain't Misbehavin' • All The Things You Are • Birdland • Body And Soul • A Foggy Day • Girl From Ipanema • Here's That Rainy Day • The Lady Is A Tramp • Love For Sale • Mercy, Mercy, Mercy • Midnight Sun • Moonlight In Vermont • Night And Day • Skylark • Stormy Weather • Sweet Georgia Brown.

00359571 ....$19.95

The Definitive Blues Collection

A massive collection of over 90 urban blues classics as well as works by legends Willie Dixon, Bessie Smith, Billie Holiday, and more. Songs include: Baby, Won't You Please Come Home • Basin Street Blues • Everyday (I Have The Blues) • Gloomy Sunday • I'm A Man • (I'm Your) Hoochie Coochie Man • Milk Cow Blues • Nobody Knows You When You're Down And Out • The Seventh Son • St. Louis Blues • The Thrill Is Gone

00311563 ....$19.95

The Definitive Rock & Roll Collection

A classic collection of the best songs from the early rock & roll years – 1955-1966. This dynamic volume contains 96 songs, including: Barbara Ann • Chantilly Lace • Dream Lover • Duke Of Earl • Earth Angel • Great Balls Of Fire • Louie, Louie • Rock Around The Clock • Ruby Baby • Runaway • (Seven Little Girls) Sitting In The Back Seat • Stay • Surfin' U.S.A. • Wild Thing • Wooly Bully • and more.

00490195 ....$19.95

For more information, see your local music dealer, or write to:

Hal Leonard Publishing Corporation

P.O. Box 13819 Milwaukee, Wisconsin 53213

Prices, contents and availability subject to change without notice.